Famous Faces
Big Book of Extreme Dot-to-Dot
From 160 to 510 Dots

By Laura's Dot to Dot Therapy

How To Use This Book

Hi! We're so glad you're a lover of puzzles and dot connecting- we are too!

Connecting the dots in this book is simple- just relax and follow the numbers in consecutive order, drawing a straight line between each one. Dot 1 will connect to dot 2 and so on and so forth until there are no more dots to connect. There's always another dot and you'll always find it. Connect every dot to discover the beautiful images they create.

In case you get lost or can't find a dot, never stress- there's an answer key at the back of the book that will show you exactly where each dot connects to the next. If you want to color your images, we encourage you to do so! Feel free to try all different colors and coloring mediums for your images!

If you find any errors or omissions in this book, just email us at Laurasdottodot@gmail.com, let us know, and we will send you a free book to make up for it! We want you to have the best dot to dot experience!

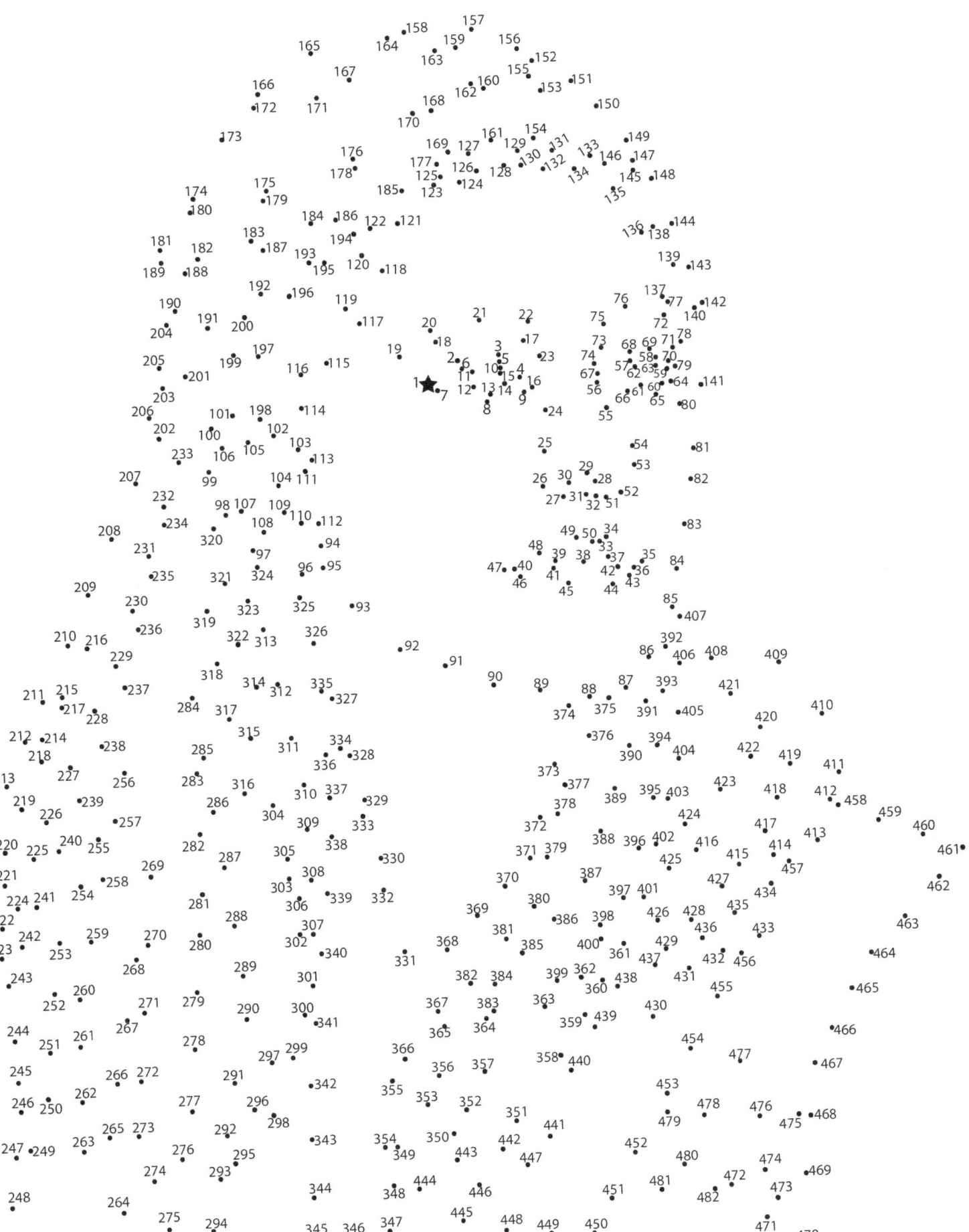

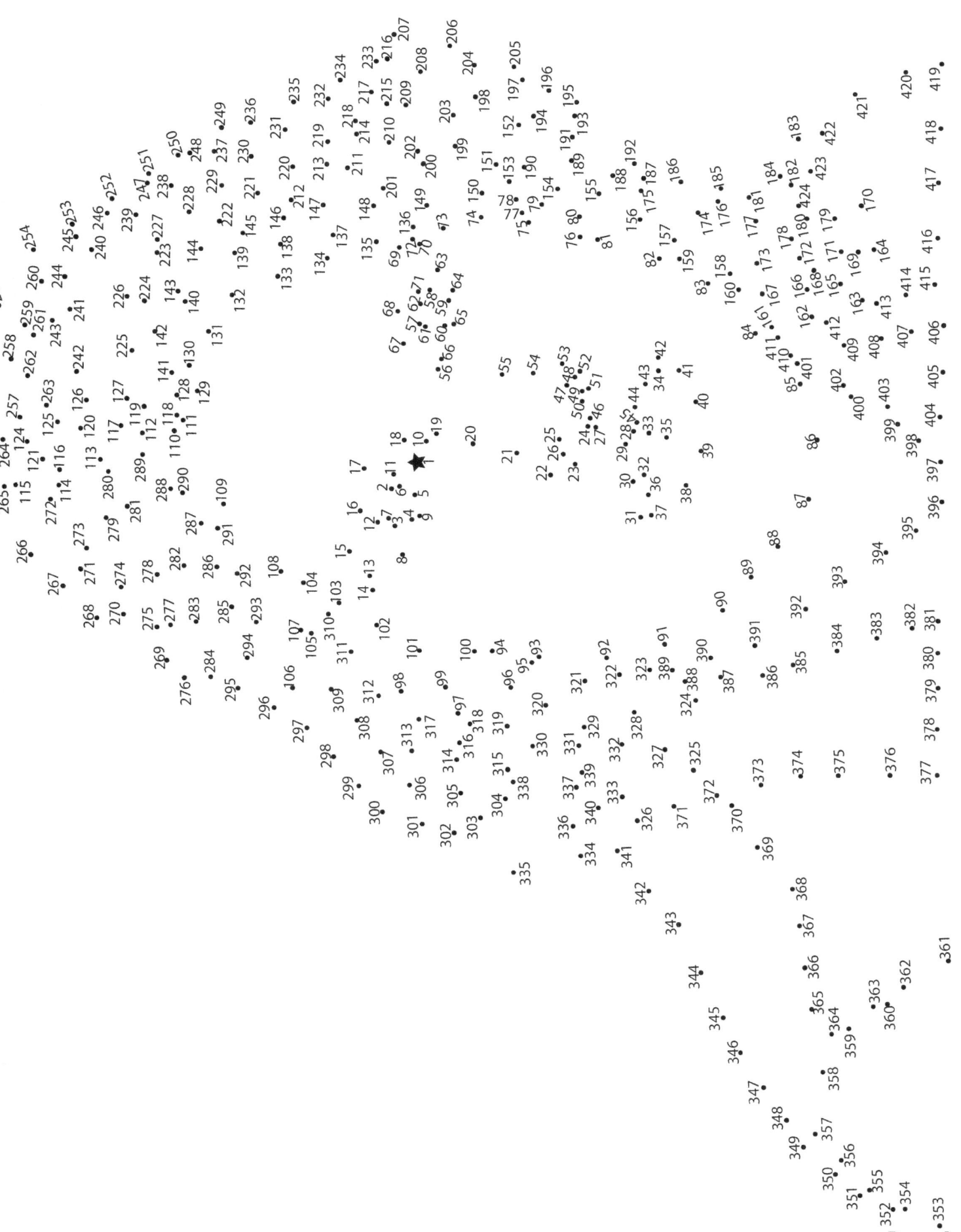

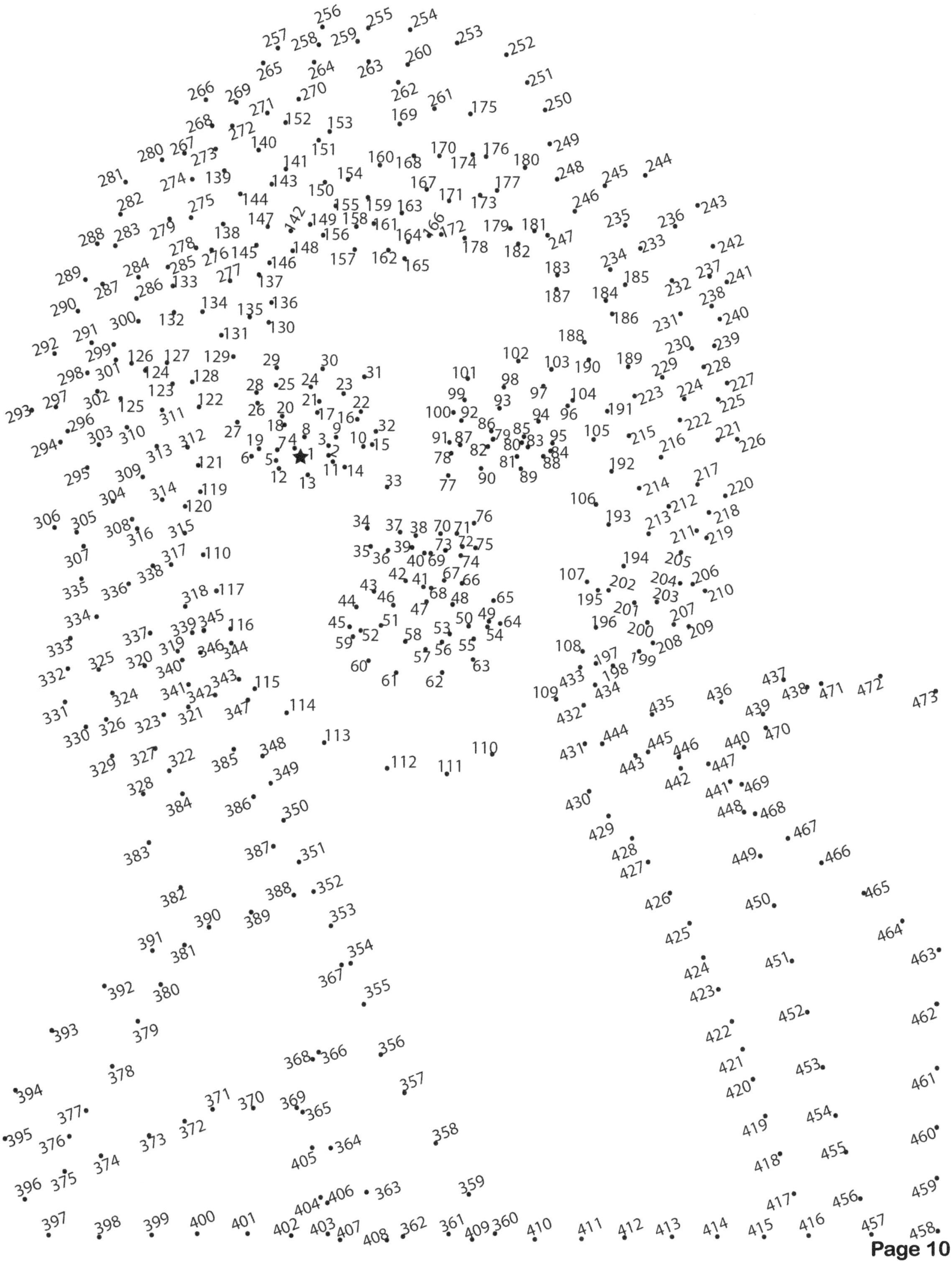

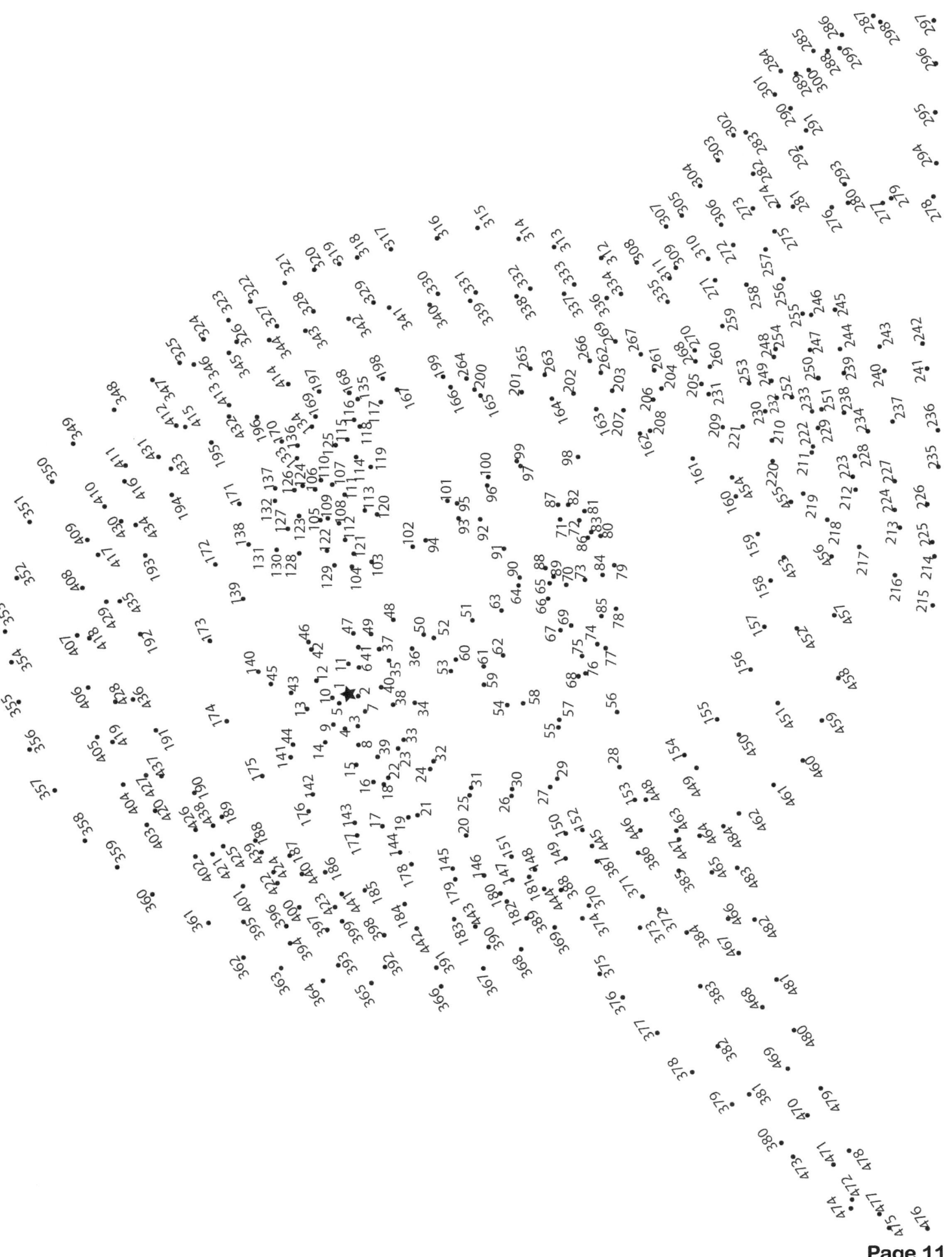

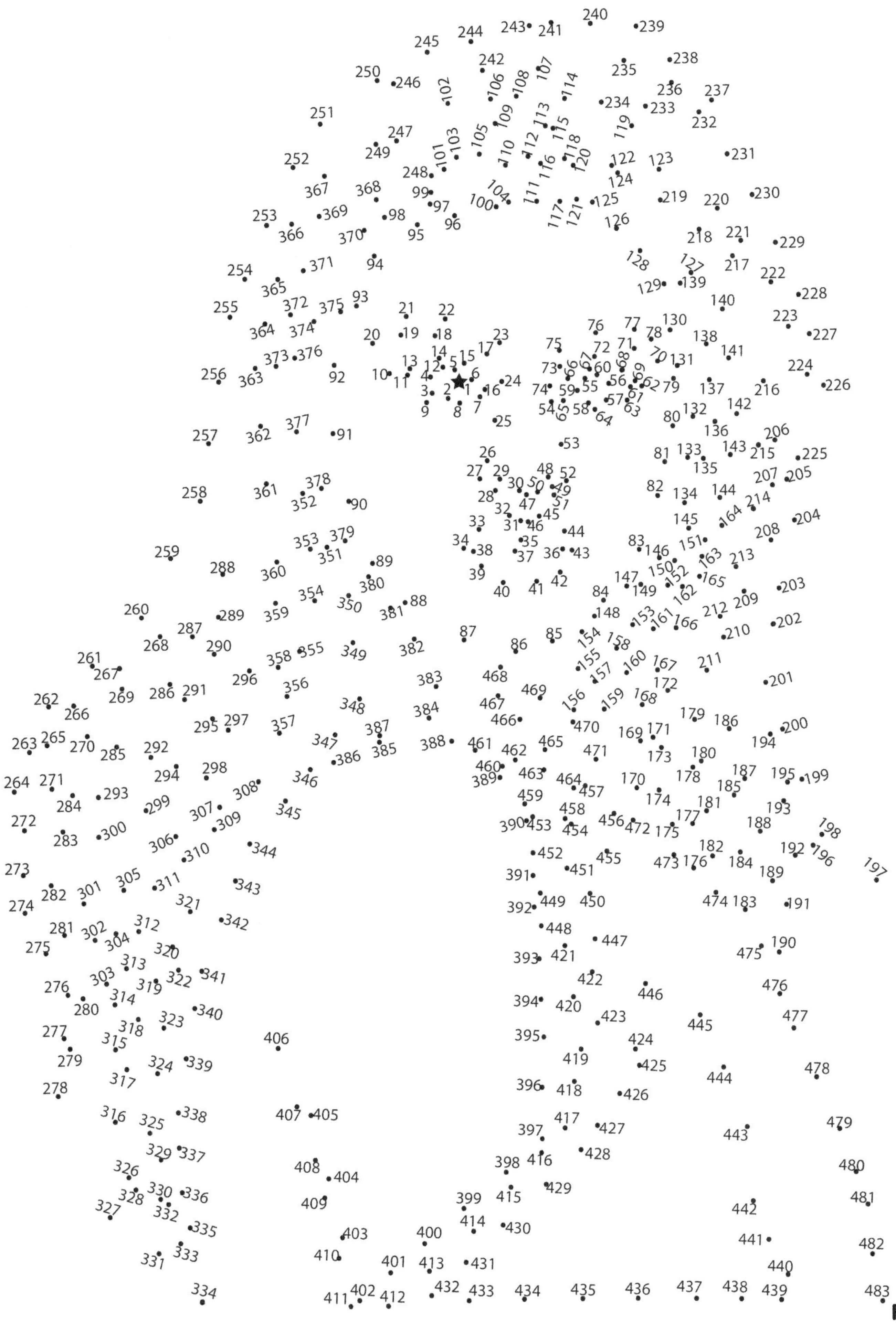

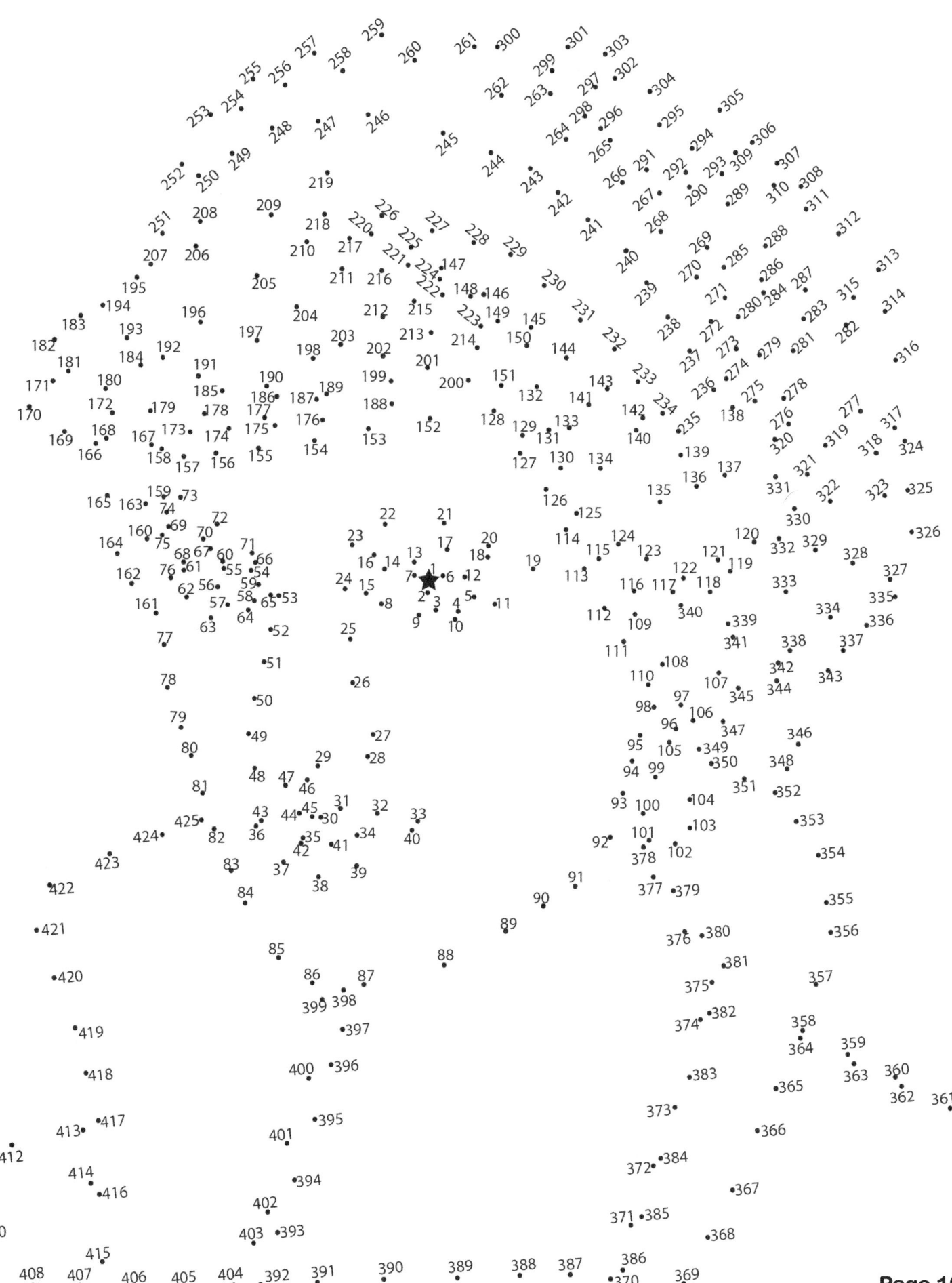

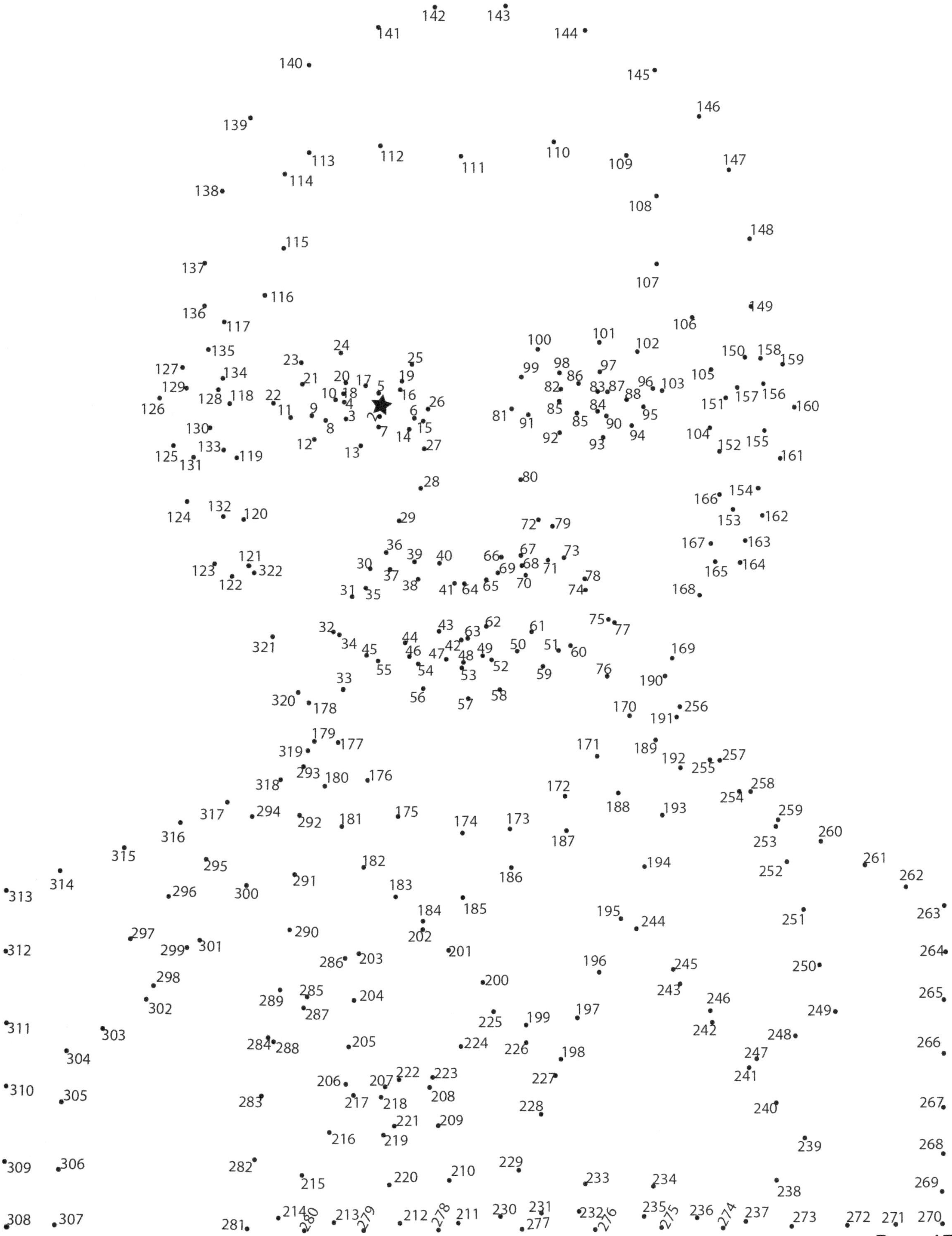

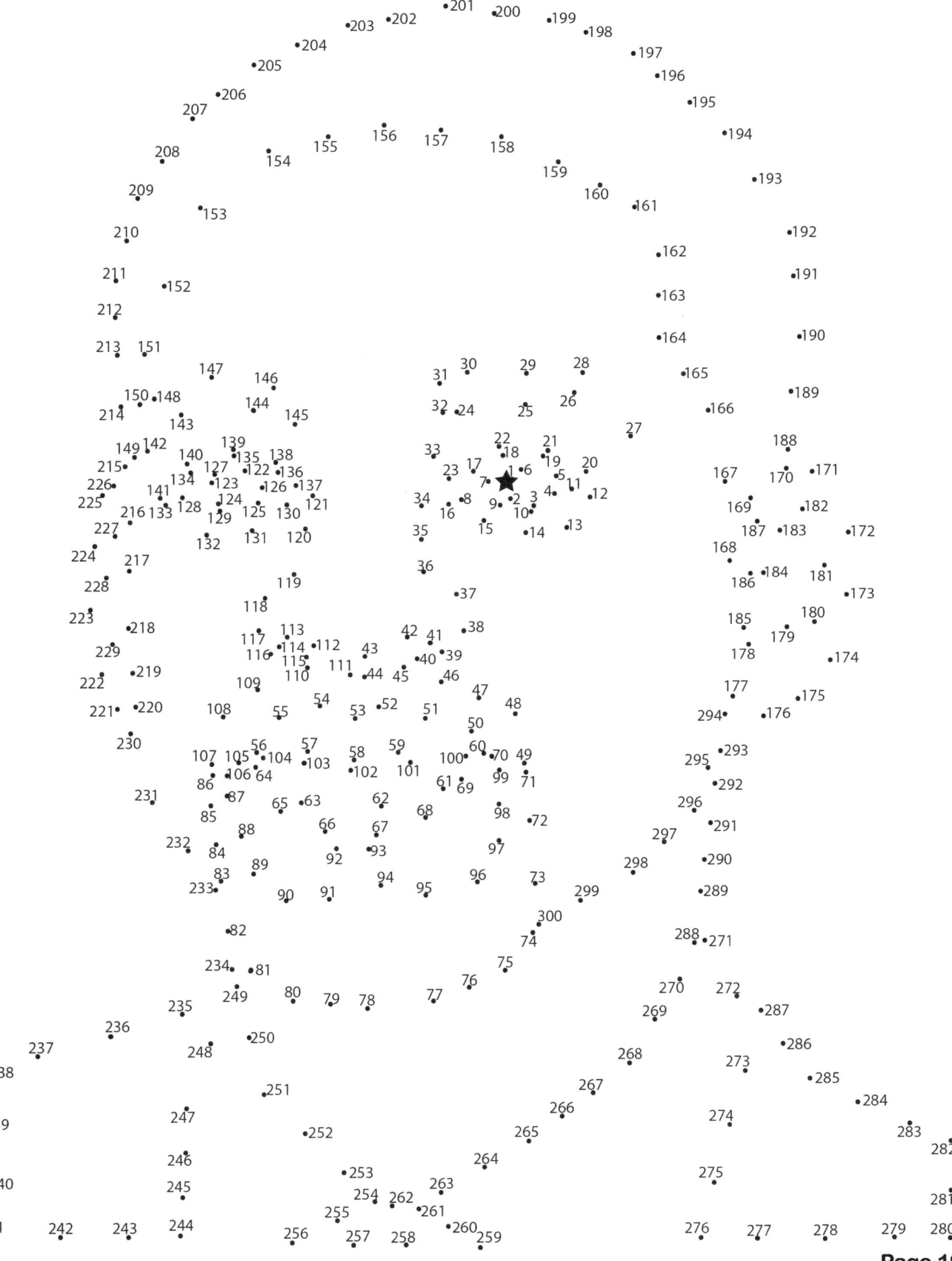

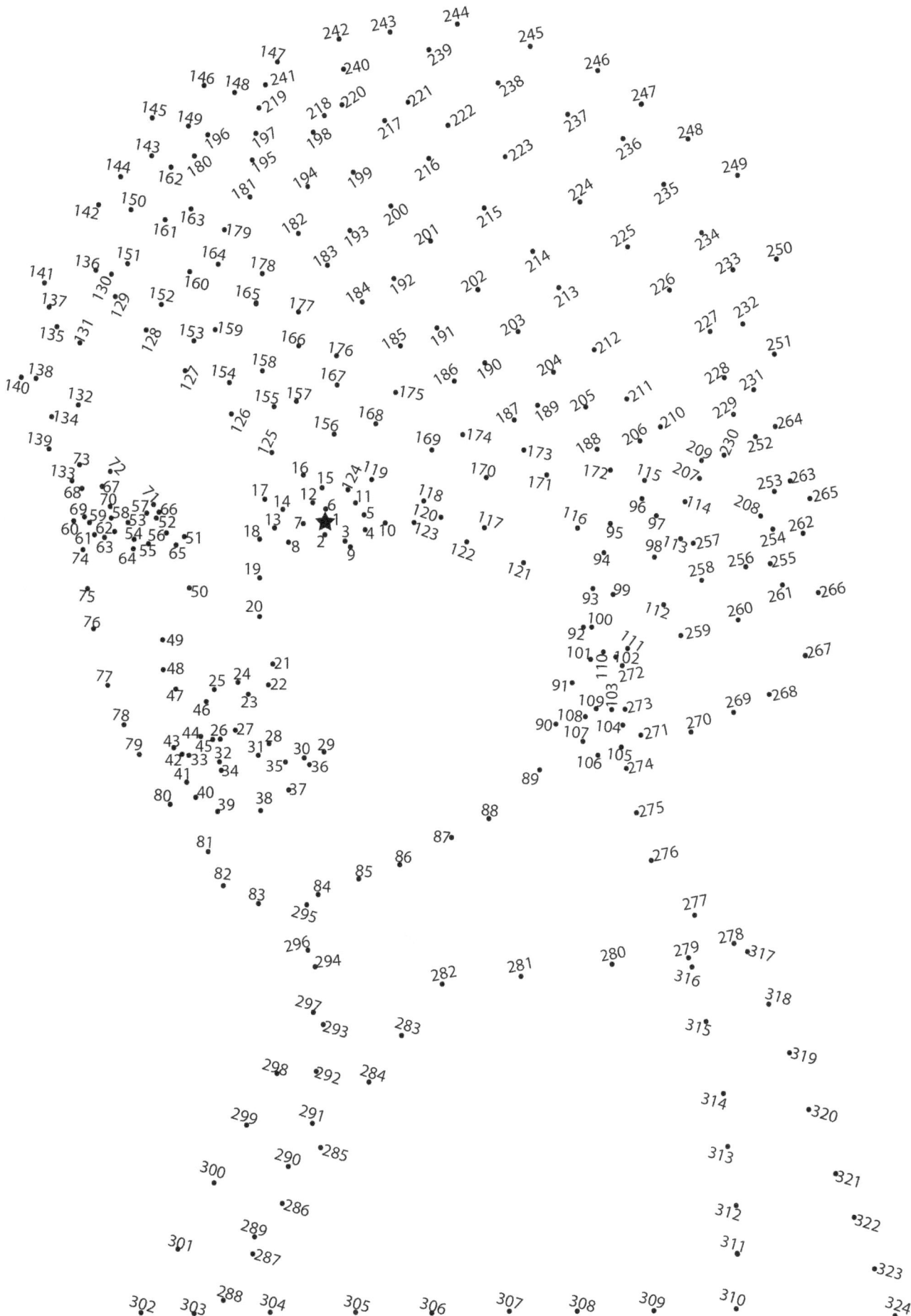

Enjoy bonus images from some of our other fun dot-to-dot books

Find all of our books on Amazon

Famous Movies and Movie Posters
Dot-to-Dot For Adults

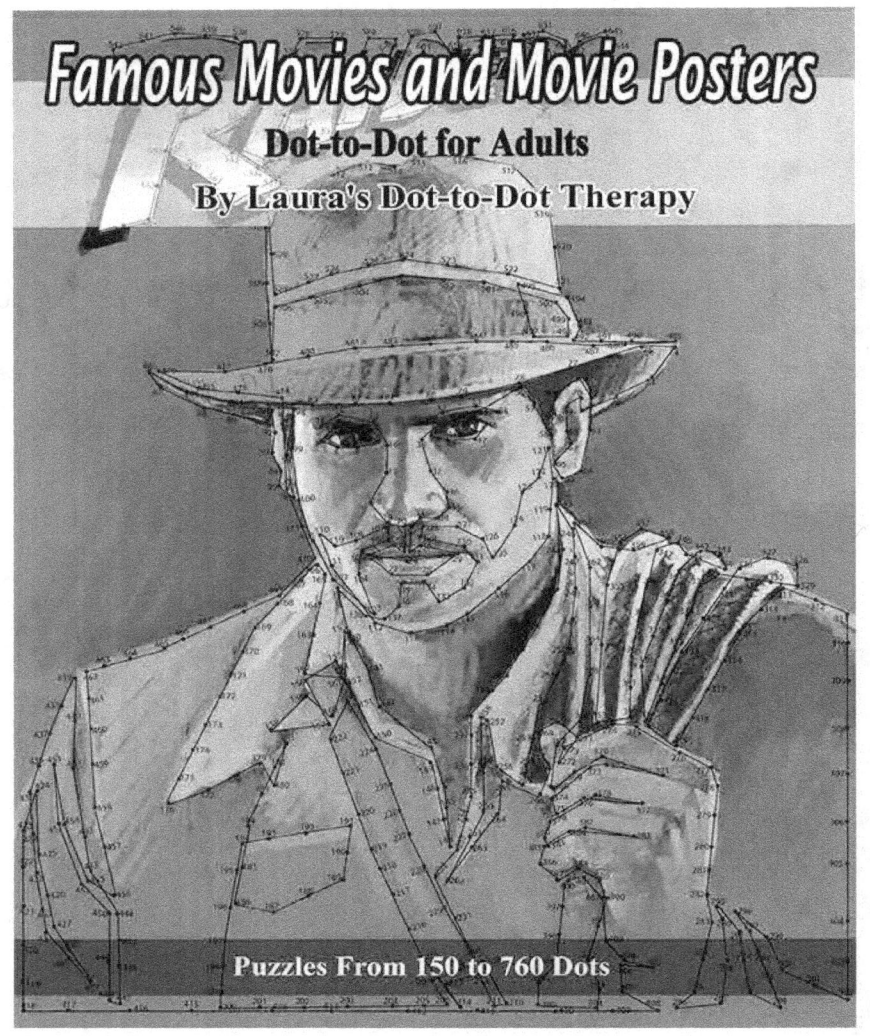

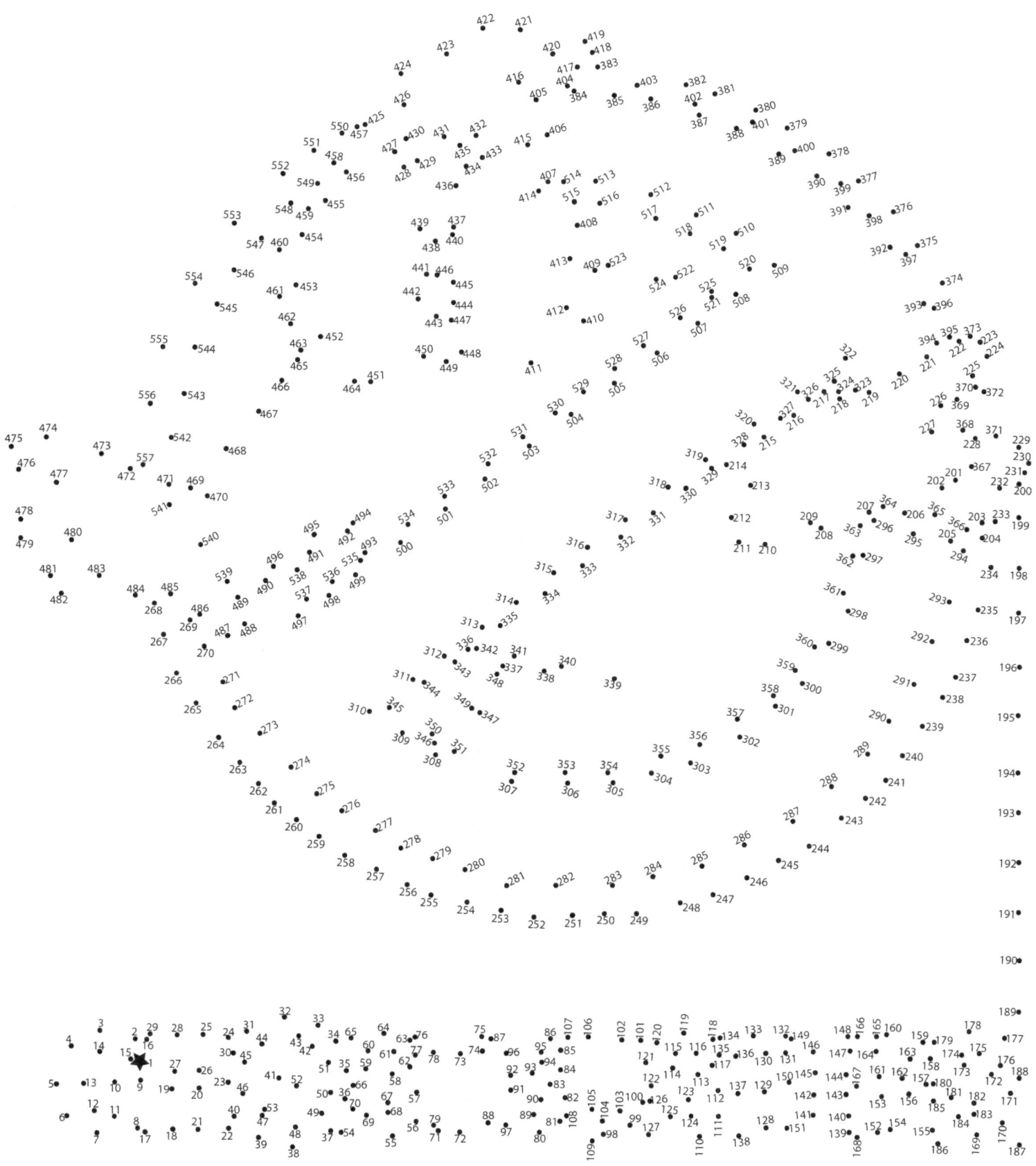

Beautiful Flowers and Butterflies
Dot-to-Dot for Adults

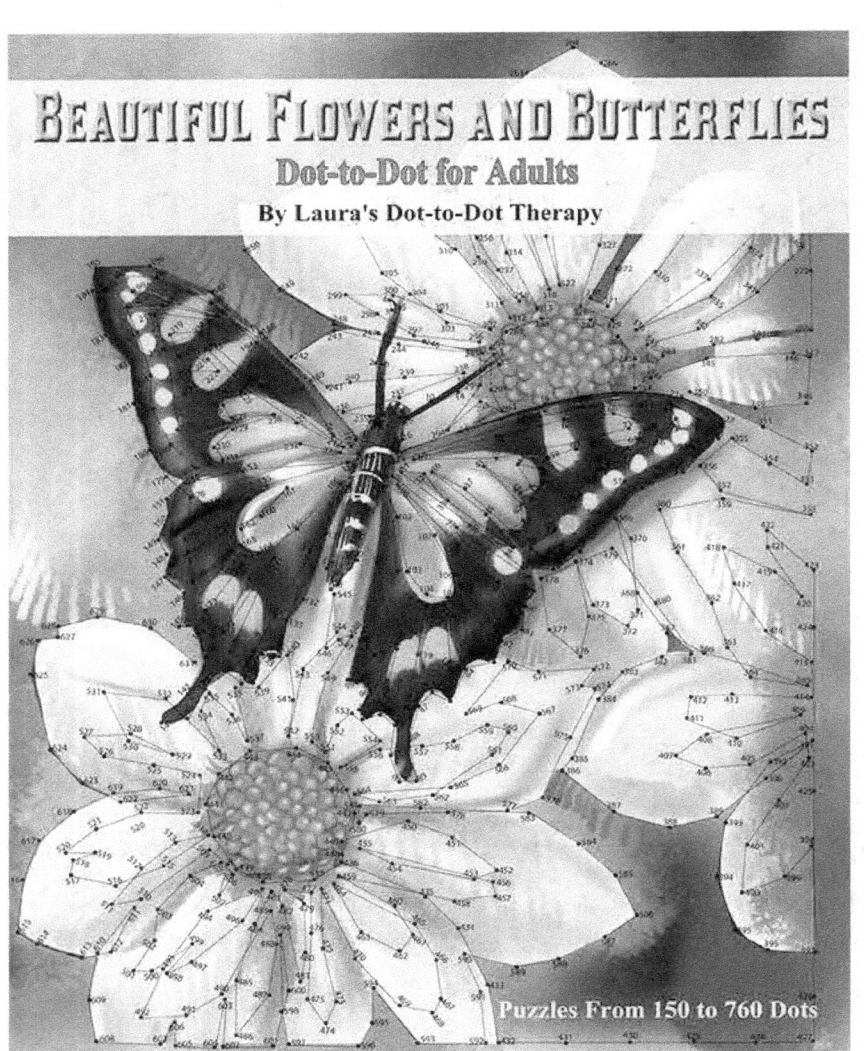

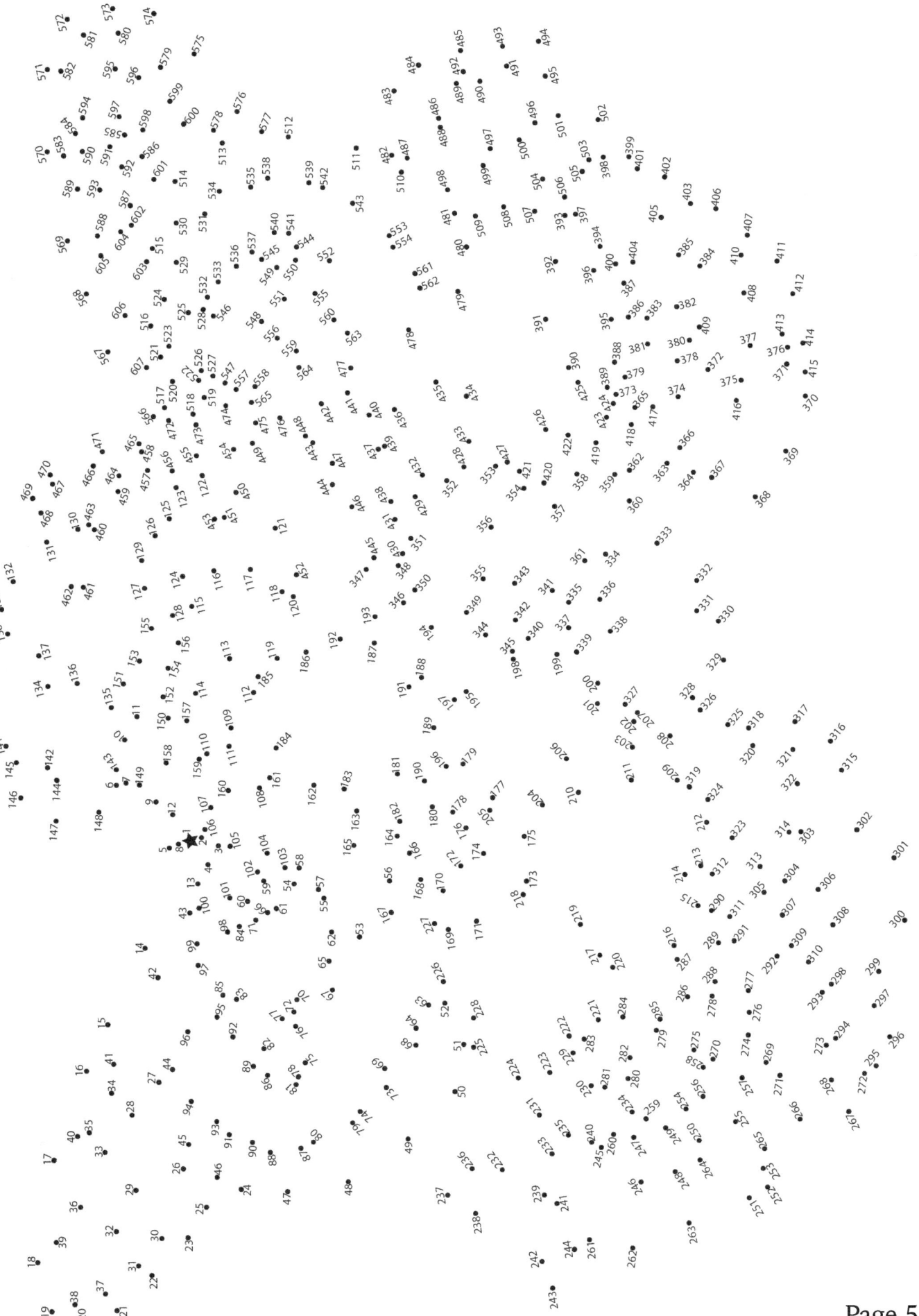

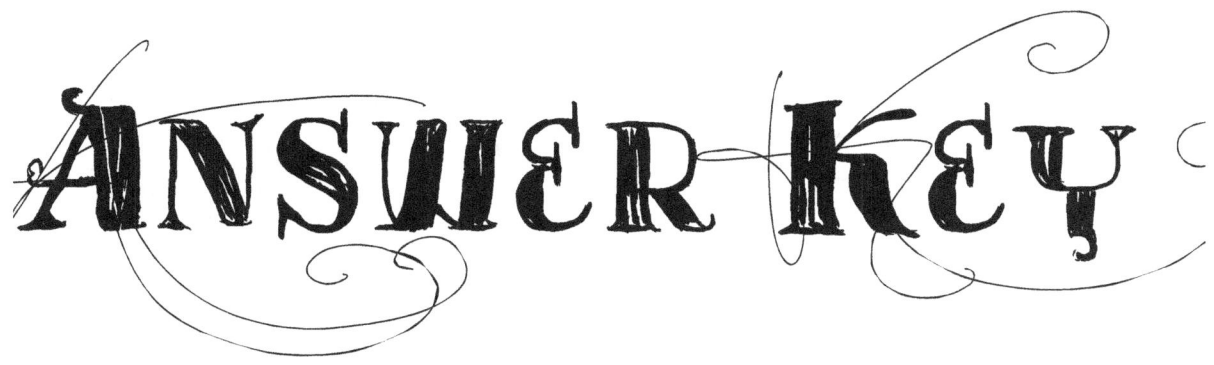

**Follow along with the
page numbers from top left
to bottom right**

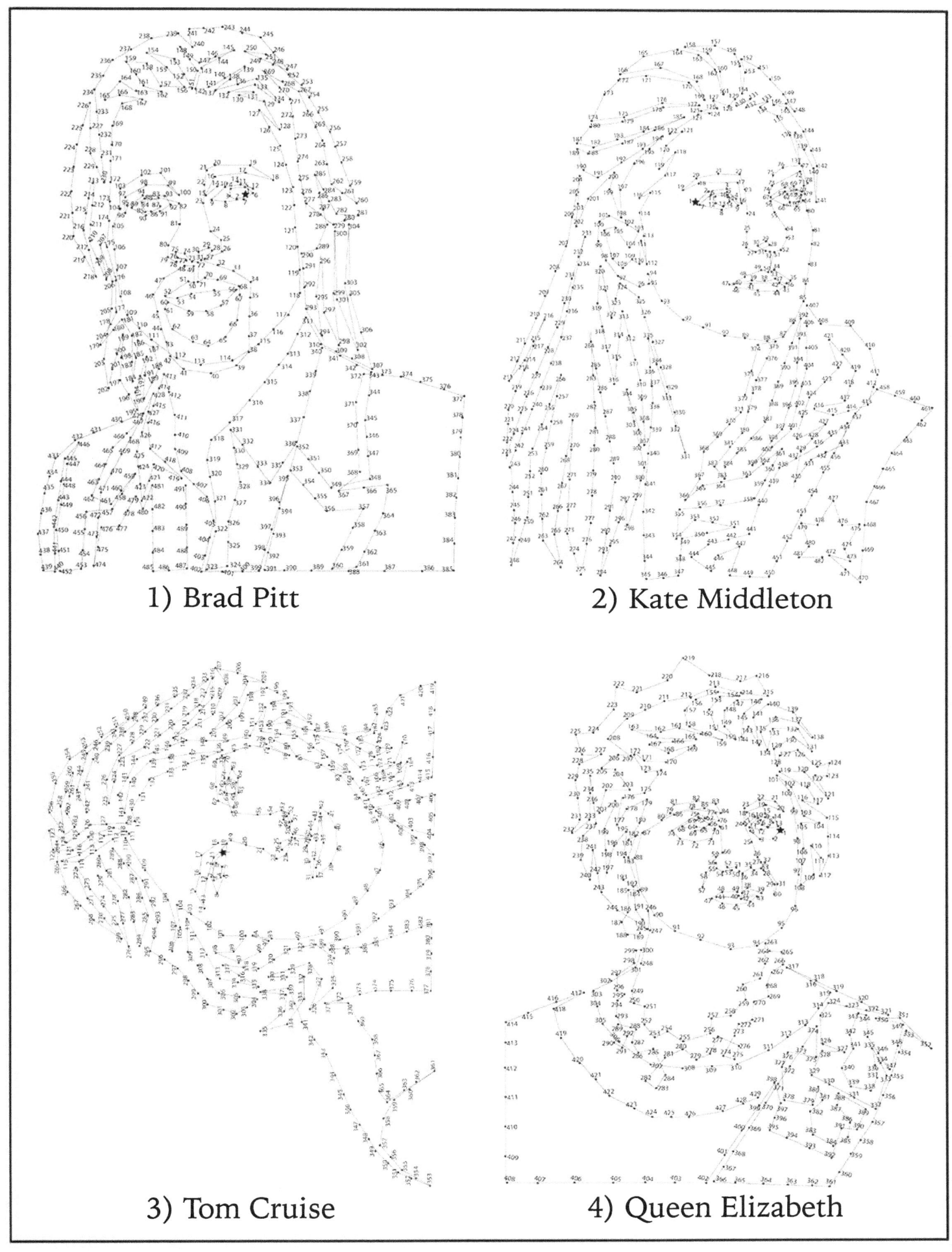

1) Brad Pitt

2) Kate Middleton

3) Tom Cruise

4) Queen Elizabeth

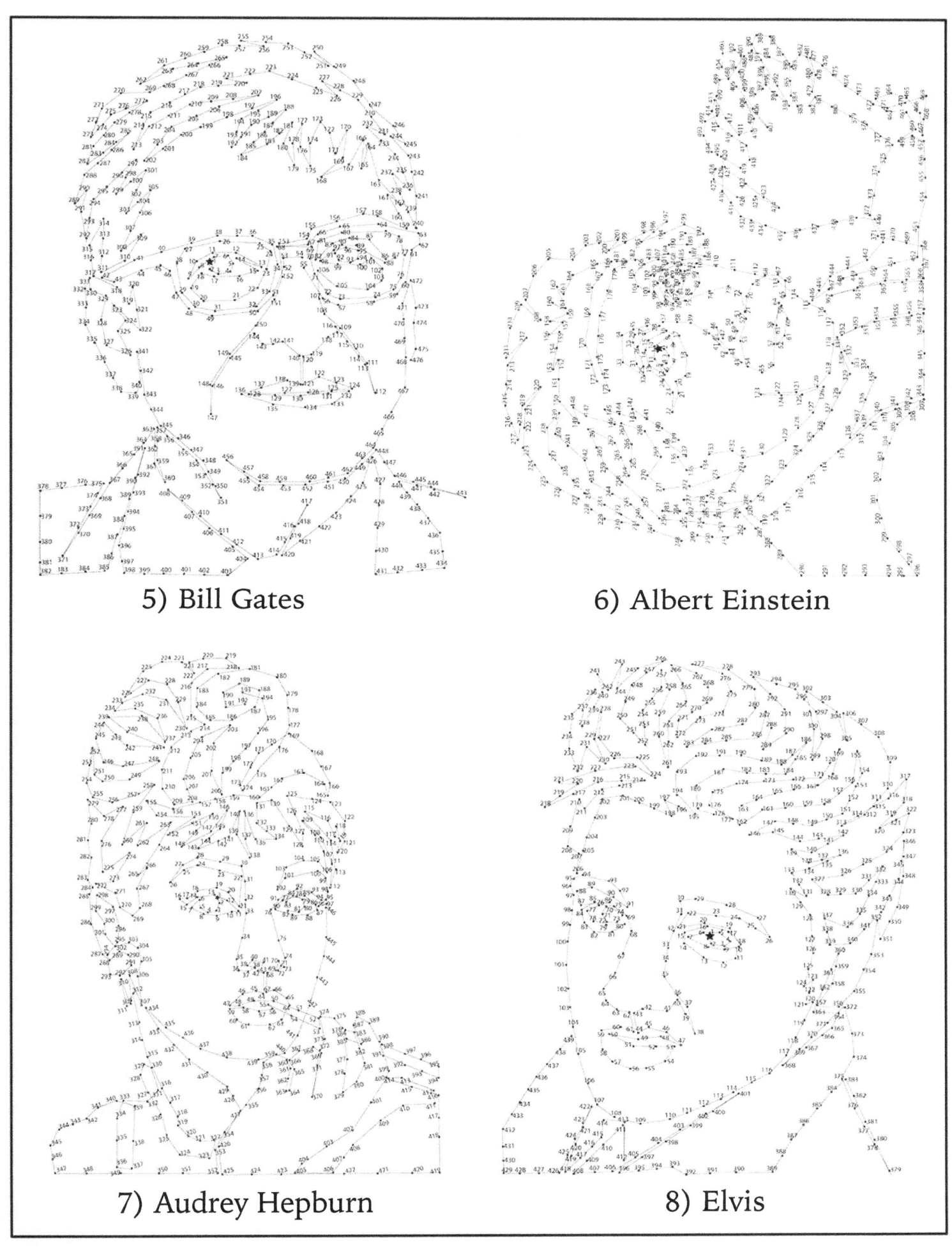

5) Bill Gates

6) Albert Einstein

7) Audrey Hepburn

8) Elvis

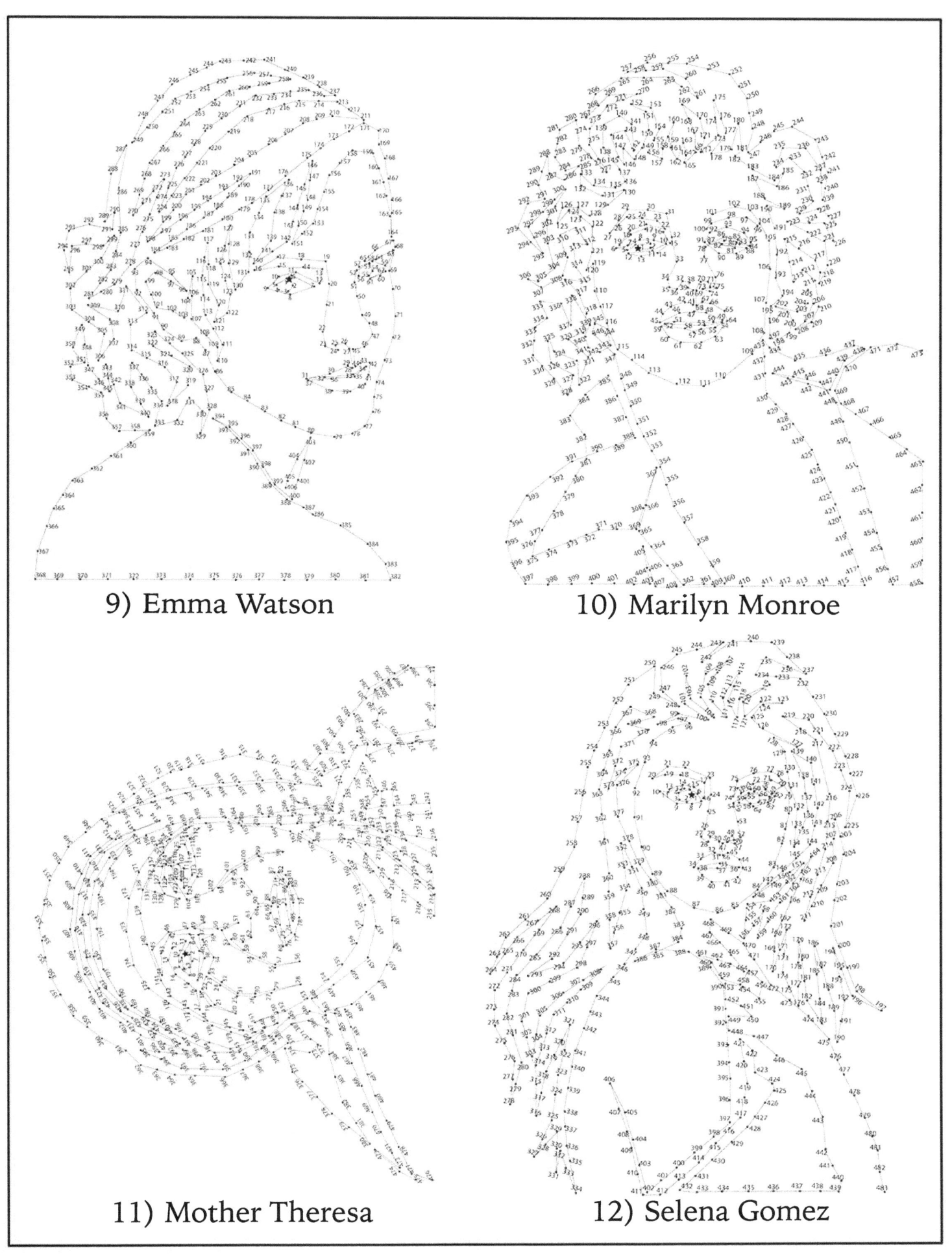

9) Emma Watson

10) Marilyn Monroe

11) Mother Theresa

12) Selena Gomez

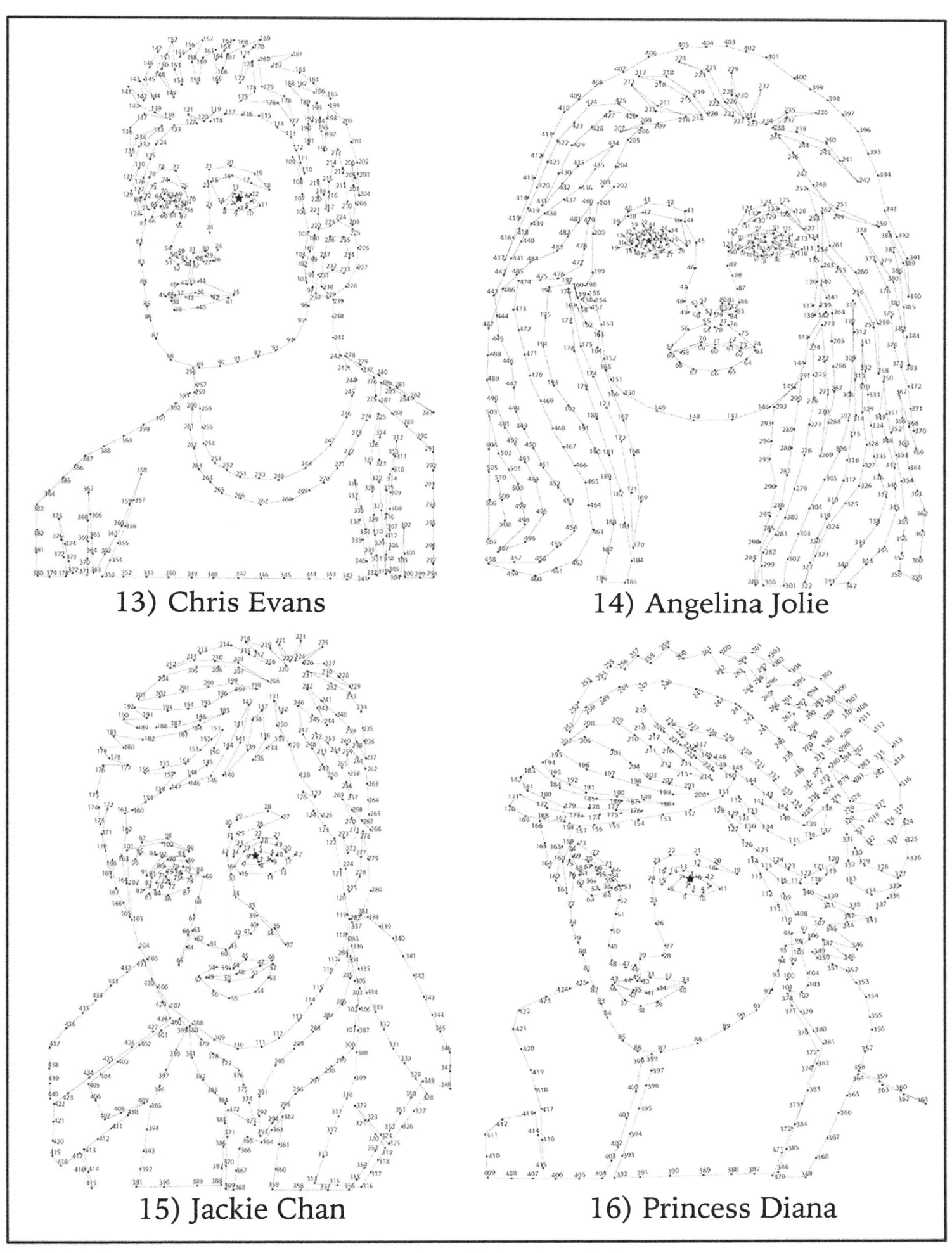

13) Chris Evans

14) Angelina Jolie

15) Jackie Chan

16) Princess Diana

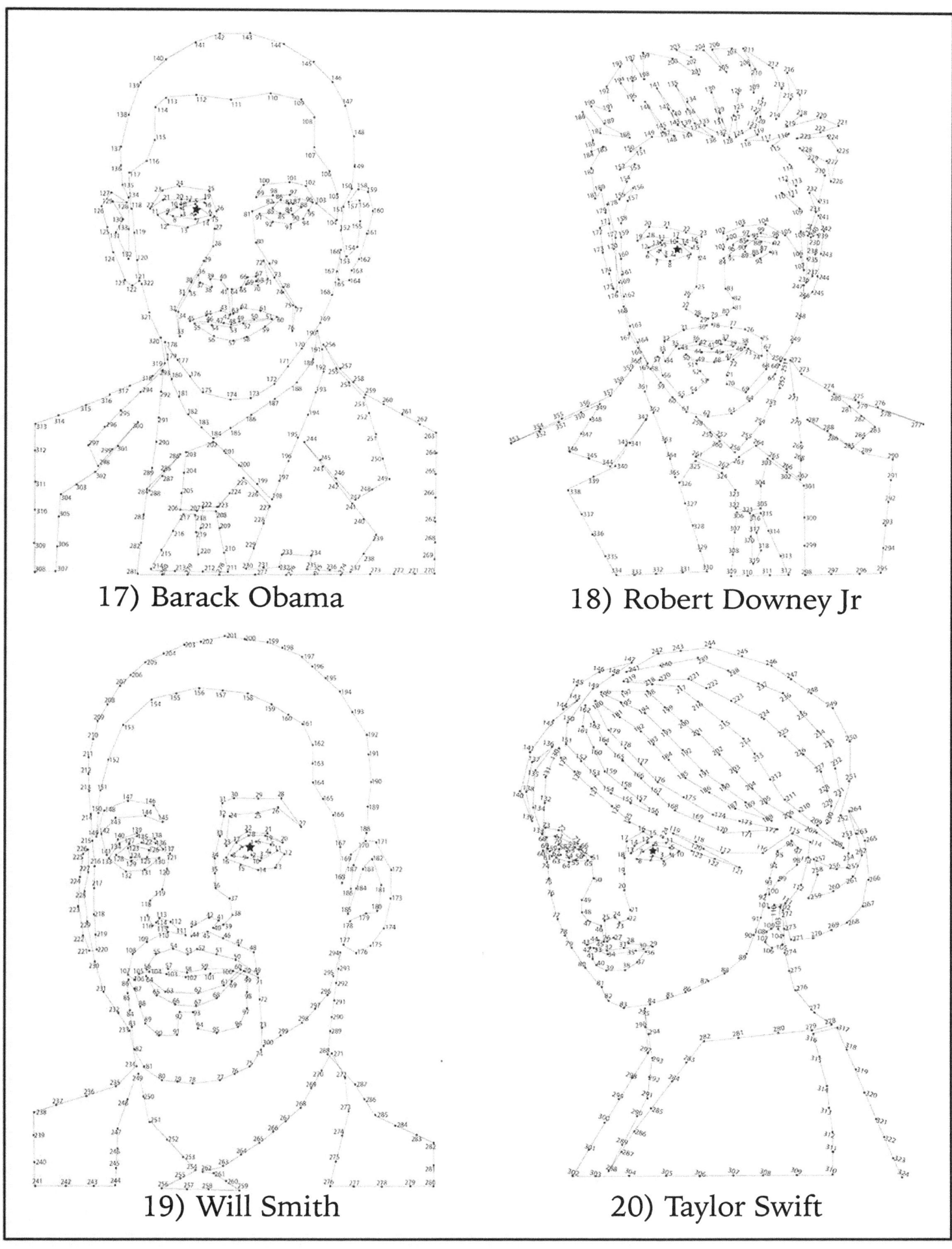

17) Barack Obama

18) Robert Downey Jr

19) Will Smith

20) Taylor Swift

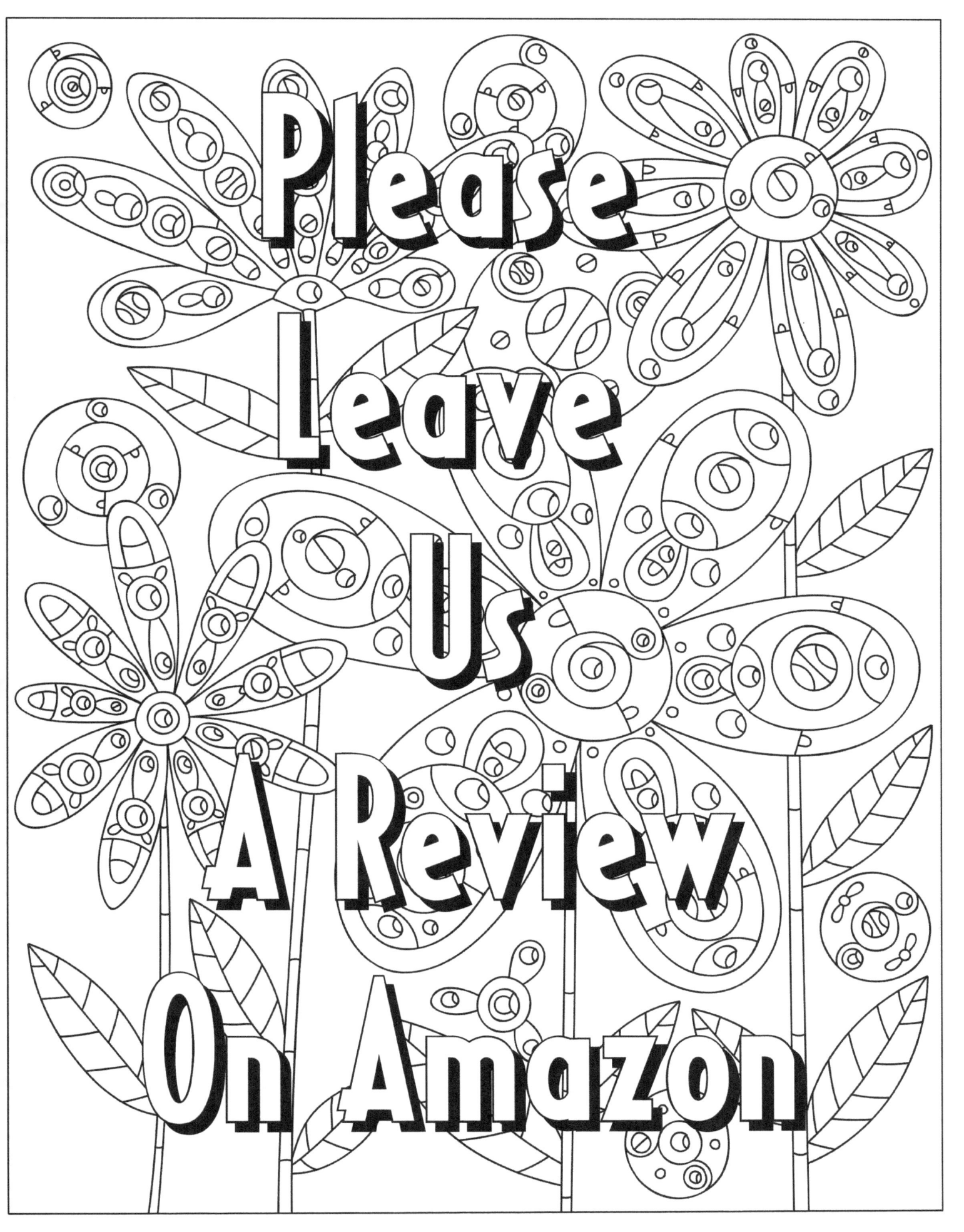

www.ingramcontent.com/pod-product-compliance
Lightning Source LLC
Chambersburg PA
CBHW081617220526
45468CB00010B/2920